A Romance
With the Master

A Romance With the Master
21 Ways to Connect With God

Teaching Guide

Karen D. Greenwell

Higgins Publishing

Oakland, CA

UNLESS OTHERWISE NOTED ALL SCRIPTURE QUOTATIONS ARE FROM THE HOLY BIBIE, NEW INTERNATIONAL VERSION. COPYRIGHT 1973, 1978, 1984 BY INTERNATIONAL BIBLE SOCIETY. USED BY PERMISSION OF ZONDERVAN PUBLISHING HOUSE, ALL RIGHTS RESERVED.

SCRIPTURE QUOTATIONS NOTED KJV ARE FROM THE KING JAMES VERSION OF THE BIBLE. SCRIPTURE QUOTATIONS noted NKJV ARE FROM THE NEW KING JAMES VERSION OF THE BIBLE. COPYRIGHT 1979, 1980, 1982. THOMAS NELSON, INC., PUBLISHERS.

HIGGINS PUBLISHING SINCE 2002

COPYRIGHT © 2015 KAREN D. GREENWELL

ALL RIGHTS RESERVED, PRINTED IN THE UNITED STATES OF AMERICA. NO PART OF THIS BOOK MAY BE USED OR REPRODUCED IN ANY MANNER WHATSOEVER WITHOUT WRITTEN PERMISSION FROM THE PUBLISHER EXCEPT IN THE CASE OF BRIEF QUOTATIONS EMBODIED IN CRITICAL ARTICLES AND REVIEWS. FOR INFORMATION EMAIL: PERMISSIONS@ HIGGINSPUBLISHING.COM.

HIGGINS PUBLISHING BOOKS MAY BE PURCHASED FOR EDUCATIONAL, BUSINESS, OR SALES PROMOTIONAL USE. FOR MORE INFORMATION EMAIL:
SPECIALMARKETS@ HIGGINSPUBLISHING.COM

LIBRARY OF CONGRESS CONTROL NUMBER: 2014943579

GREENWELL, KAREN D. A ROMANCE WITH THE MASTER TEACHING GUIDE / KAREN D. GREENWELL

ISBN 978-1-9415801-7-2 (PB)

HIGGINS PUBLISHING, ITS LOGOS AND MARKS ARE SERVICE MARKS OF HIGGINS PUBLISHING.

HTTP://WWW.HIGGINSPUBLISHING.COM

COVER ILLUSTRATION BY: LISBEL GAVARA MONFORT
BACK COVER PHOTO BY: GRANT JOHNSTON
PRINTED ON ECO-FRIENDLY PAPER

Contents

How to Use This Guide — Page vii

Session One: Lessons 1 and 2 — Page 13

Session Two: Lessons 3 and 4 — Page 27

Session Three: Lessons 5, 6, and 7 — Page 37

Session Four: Lessons 8, 9, 10, and 11 — Page 45

Session Five: Lessons 12, 13, and 14 — Page 55

Session Six: Lessons 15, 16, and 17 — Page 61

Session Seven: Lessons 18, 19, 20, and 21 — Page 71

Session Eight: Final Discussion — Page 81

How to Use This Teaching Guide

Welcome to the teaching guide for *A Romance With the Master: 21 Ways to Connect With God.* I would like to assume that you have the heart and desire to teach, equip, and enable women to be all that God desires them to be because you have purchased this teaching guide.

My own heart for teaching women has grown through the many years of my own trials, as well as observing girls and women struggle to find out who they really are. In this day and age, I believe it is even more important for women to step into the places that God has for them. Women need to be free from fear and to be able to find the ultimate love that only Jesus Christ can give.

This guide has been written to assist you, as a group leader or Bible study teacher, with the lessons in *A Romance With the Master.* Please feel free to use whatever you find useful in the Bible study or the guide. I have provided as much information as I can so that, following this guide, you can teach the lessons in the same way that I do.

I have adapted this guide from my own lessons as I teach *A Romance With the Master*. Throughout this Bible study it would be fairly easy to put together lessons, but each lesson has a particular idea or thought that I believe needs to be stressed. The lessons you will find here are all of the lessons that I teach, with the added information that I believe you should use in order to stress the main idea.

Each lesson is formatted and highlighted based on how I teach it, providing you an optional guide to lesson flow. The sections in brackets supplement the lessons with directions or additional information on key points. The information inside the brackets is for your use only, unless you choose otherwise.

This guide is designed for small Bible study groups, say 5 to 7 people. For larger groups, the whole group can be

How To Use This Teaching Guide

divided into smaller groups, each with their own leader, for the prayer and discussion sections.

Here are some tips to help you as you teach this Bible study:

1. Dare to believe that women can be healed and set free and be all that God has called them to be.
2. Pray for the women in your group daily.
3. Invite all women to join your Bible study group. Do not limit your invitations to single women or single mothers. Many married women have expectations of their human husbands that need to be placed in Christ.
4. Stay in contact with your group members during the week to let them know that you are thinking of them and praying for them.
5. Prepare for teaching this study ahead of time by reading and doing the lessons yourself.

6. Commit to your own personal growth in Christ. Use the 21 Ways for yourself.

I designed the format of the Bible study book so that it can be used as a workbook, as well as read as a book. The workbook is designed to be written in, both on the lines or in the margins. There are quite a few questions or readings that will be personal, so when each woman in your group has her own book, she can use and write in it personally, and refer back to it as needed.

The teaching of the lessons for each session should be ahead of the reading and answering the questions for those lessons. Then each woman can take her own time reading the lessons and answering questions before the next session. When the main ideas are presented during the teaching, the women can take notes, and know what to look for as they read each lesson on their own.

I have designed the Bible study to be about 90 minutes long with extra time for more discussion as desired.

How To Use This Teaching Guide

Time tags are given for each section and lesson. Allow 15 to 20 minutes to teach a lesson if a time tag is not given due to lack of space.

Page numbers in brackets are for reference and are the page numbers in the Bible study workbook. The general format for the sessions, except for the first session, should be as follows:

1. Opening prayer. I have not provided "canned" prayers here. Please pray as you see fit for your group.
2. Discussion of questions from last week's lessons. The reading of the scriptures with the questions may be done by you, or you can have one of your group read them. I have provided ample time for discussion questions as most of the lessons will not take as long as indicated.

3. Teaching of the new lessons. With the extra time allowed, you are free to add as much content as you like.

4. Closing prayer. Again, no "canned" prayers here; feel free to have a time of ministry as well.

I pray that God will use you for His glory as you teach this Bible study. Be blessed as you learn and teach this study. And do not forget to relax and have some fun, too.

Session One: Lessons 1 and 2

Opening prayer 1 to 2 minutes

Introductions 1 to 2 minutes each

1. The teacher or leader first.
2. Others in the group, one at a time.

A Little Background 10 minutes

1. Read *A Romance With the Master*, page 23. [If you have a similar experience to mine on page 23, please share it instead of mine. The main idea is that God gave me Isaiah 54:4-17, and told me He was my husband after my divorce and I took Him at His word, literally. Encourage the women to do the same as they begin their romance with the Master.]

2. We still live in a society that sees a single woman as incomplete. It is a society that still expects women to depend on men for their needs, even though many women now take care of themselves and their

families. God the Father, Jesus Christ the Son, and the Holy Spirit should be all we need for everything in our lives. [see *A Romance With the Master*, Preface, page XIII.]

3. We do not need a man to complete us, we need God:
   a. Our deepest insecurities cannot be filled by others, not even a mate.
   b. Find the ultimate love and security you desire in God.
4. The theme of the study is "finding security in God." We cannot be secure until we trust God. We cannot trust God unless we believe what He says and we cannot believe what He says until we know who He is. This is Know-Believe-Trust: 7 steps to know God, 7 things He tells us to believe, and 7 aspects of trusting Him.

Session One: Lessons 1 and 2

Teaching

LESSON 1: I AM ON THE LINE   15 minutes

Read Isaiah 54:4, page 25.

Fear Not, God is calling you just where you are, in whatever situation you find yourself. [Stress that we are afraid because we are facing scary circumstances (Joshua 1:6-9), or we are afraid because we do not know what the future holds (1 Kings 17:7-16), or maybe something miraculous is about to happen (Luke 1:26-33).]

Do not be afraid; God is trying to get your attention! God uses your circumstances to get your attention. He wants you to start looking for Him.

When you are afraid, or when you are in a bad place, God is calling you. He is calling you because He wants you to begin to get to know Him, or know Him better.

He calls you first, He loves you first. God's perfect love, when you know how much He loves you, will cast out all of your fears. But you have to begin to acknowledge your fears.

In-Class Exercise: 10 minutes

Take 5 to 10 minutes to think about your deepest fears. Prioritize them and write them in the list on page 29. [The Fear List does not need to be all "big" fears. The idea is for the women to put some of their fears in order from greatest to least. We will refer back to this list later.]

Fear is overcome by love, 1 John 4:18. It is God's perfect love that will cast out all of our fears. It is this same perfect love that He showed us when He sacrificed His Son on the cross for us.

When you know that you know that God loves you, nothing else matters. Do you know how much He loves you? Do you know how much He wants you to respond to Him?

Start growing your faith in God. [Page 32] Jesus said a tiny mustard seed of faith would move mountains.

Session One: Lessons 1 and 2

You have to start with a small amount of faith first. [Faith is like a muscle; it has to be exercised in order to grow.]

But too often you may expect Big Things with your tiny faith only to have your expectations dashed. You may have some left over big prayers that have not been answered yet. Do you believe God will answer your prayers?

Faith must start with the small things, like praying for $20 for gas, or for your water bill to be paid, not necessarily praying for a new car or a new house (worth more monetarily). Or maybe start with smaller spiritual and emotional prayers such as patience with other drivers, or not to lose your temper over small things, rather than prayers that ask God to make you perfect tomorrow, or that world hunger will end tomorrow.

God really does care about the little things in your life. He wants you to start there. Too often, you may have the idea that God only cares about the big things and that He does not want you to bother Him with the small things. NO!

God wants you to surrender everything; He wants to be in control of everything, right down to your toes. God is in the details.

Read Matthew 25:14-30 Parable of the Talents. [Discuss the intended meaning of this passage that if we are faithful in the few things, we will be made responsible for many things.]

God follows His own Biblical laws. God Himself will follow this same pattern that He gives in the parable of the talents. He will show Himself faithful to us in the small things first, then we can begin to believe Him and trust Him more for the big things.

Can we rephrase the scripture? If God is faithful in the small things, then we will make Him ruler over everything in our lives. [As God answers the little prayers, our faith in Him grows so that we can begin to believe Him for the bigger things.]

In-Class Exercise: 10 minutes

Take 5 to 10 minutes to think about your needs. Prioritize your needs and write them in the list on page 35. [Again, they do not all have to be "big" needs. The women should just prioritize some of their needs, in order, number 1 being the greatest and number 5 being the least.]

Your first tiny step of faith is to believe that God loved you first and that He is calling to you! Surrender to His call; Fear Not!

Pray the fear/need prayer on page 37 together. [Stress that the women are praying for their **smallest** fears and needs. These are the ones to start with. You might want to have each woman bow her head and pray it silently because she may not want to share the things on her list with the group. Encourage the women to share next week any answers to this prayer.]

LESSON 2: I ALREADY KNOW YOU   15 minutes

Read Isaiah 54:4 again, page 39.

God knows all about you, down to the last detail. He knows your past and present and future. He says you will not suffer shame or disgrace because of your trust in Him.

God knows how you feel, [Page 40] especially when you are in a bad situation or circumstances. But, sometimes your feelings can be wrong and even if they are wrong, God still knows how you feel.

Just because something "feels" right does not mean it necessarily is. Faith and feelings are not the same things. God sees your heart and He cares about how you feel, but He wants you to believe Him more than trust your feelings.

You must surrender your feelings of shame, disgrace, regret, and humiliation to Him. And any other issues that interfere with your faith and cause you to doubt.

[These are some of the small things to begin to believe that God will take care of.]

He says you will not be disgraced: wounded, taunted, or confused. [Page 43] God knows when you are questioning your circumstances or wondering what He is doing in your life. [There are two types of shame: the shame we have when we have done something or someone wrong, and then the shame others try to put on us in order to boost themselves up. God deals with both of these types of shame, the first starting on page 39, and the second starting on page 45.]

What the author calls the Prayer-Convince process is praying over and over again about something you are worrying about or cannot stop thinking about. You continue to pray for the same problem, not out of lack of faith, but because *you* will eventually be convinced that God really is in control.

God knows what you are asking; He is at work, but if you are thinking and worrying about it then you need to keep giving it to Him. [I finally put a name to this kind of prayer when I wrote the Bible study. I was a basket case after my divorce, thinking and worrying about one thing all day long and I learned firsthand to give it to God in prayer *every time* I thought about it.]

We keep praying over and over for the same thing until *we* are convinced that God will answer; *not* because He is hard of hearing. [This is the type of prayer to use to eventually be free of shame, disgrace, regret, and humiliation.]

God knows when others are trying to shame or humiliate you. You just keep surrendering your feelings and situations to Him. Keep your eyes on God, not on what others are doing.

He will take care of things. No one can affect your feelings when you have surrendered them to God.

God says you will forget the shame of your youth. [Page 46] God knows your past and all the dumb things you may have done. He sees the skeletons in your closet. Open wide that closet door and let Him have them all.

He knows any regrets you may have about whatever. Let the Blood of Jesus Christ wash over you and cleanse away your regrets as you give them to Him. And if you keep remembering them, use the prayer-convince process.

You will remember no more any reproach of widowhood. [Page 48] Whether you are single or married or widowed in this life, when you are hidden away in God and have surrendered to Him, there is no more reproach and you will not remember any shame you may have had in the past. And you do not have to be ashamed for where you are now.

When you are secure in Christ and in the knowledge of His great love for you, you are sheltered from any storm, you are confident in His love.

God knows that you may have a hole in your heart: A God space. [Page 49] This is the place in your heart that cannot be filled by anyone except God. This is the place where you may be the most insecure. [My deepest insecurities were the ones I was trying to put on other people.]

God did not design us to carry other people's deep insecurities. Only He can carry these deep insecurities, and He wants to.

Let God romance you. Let Him fill those vacant spaces with His love for you. Let Him sweep you off your feet. Do not be afraid to be carried away by His love. Let Him replace your insecurities with confidence in Christ alone.

Pray the last prayer of surrender together on page 50. [Make sure the women understand that they are to read Lessons 1 and 2, do the required scripture reading, and answer the questions in both lessons before the next session.

Do not tell them ahead of time which questions will be discussed next session. This will be the pattern for all the sessions.]

Ministry Time/Closing Prayer.

Session Two: Lessons 3 and 4

Opening Prayer 1 to 2 minutes

Lesson 1 Discussion Questions 20 minutes

    a. Question #1, page 26, read the scripture, then answer the question.

    b. Question #4, page 28, read the scripture, then answer the question.

Lesson 2 Discussion Questions 20 minutes

    a. Question #2, page 41, read Psalm 22, then answer the question.

    b. Question #3, page 27, read the scripture, then answer the question

    c. Question #4, page 43, read the scripture, then answer the question.

    d. Fear/Need Lists: would anyone like to share answered prayer from your Fear/Need lists.

Teaching

LESSON 3: I AM THE GENERAL WHO RESCUES

Read Isaiah 54:5, page 51.

When two people are introduced, they usually exchange names, what they do for a living, and possibly their job titles. And then, as they spend more time together, they get know their reactions, emotions, and character qualities.

God is now going to introduce Himself to you.

God is your maker. [Page 51] He created you to be the real person you are, exactly how you look, with all of your personality traits and quirks.

You are in His thoughts. You are not an accident, even if your parents thought you were. God planned you from the very beginning of time.

God created you to be His bride, His lover, His wife. That is why He wants to romance you. He wants to love you as you were created to be loved.

God is wooing you. He longs for your heart. He longs to be the one that you run to, snuggle into, and depend on for everything.

God says He is your husband. Webster's dictionary defines a husband as a "prudent or frugal manager" and to "husband" is to "till or cultivate." God is the husband who is gentle, caring, and He will do whatever it takes to have a fruitful and loving wife. This means you!

What does having a husband mean to you? [The following sections are from the book under the same section headings. If you can think of any more and want to add them, by all means, do so.]

Are you looking for a man to be your security? [Page 55] God is the God of the universe; He sees everything and everybody. He knows everything and everybody. He already know the plans He has for you, and your future. He will carry out those plans, if you let Him. When you learn to trust Him and that He really does know what He is doing, then you can rest in His peace. You can be secure in Him.

Are you looking for a man to be your companion? [Page 56] What is a companion? Someone who just hangs out with you or keeps you company? What better companion than Someone who already knows you, loves you, wants to spend time with you, and is available 24/7?

Are you looking for a man to be your lover? [Page 57] Jesus Christ is the ultimate lover. You must totally surrender to Him to be in complete union with Him. He is the only Man who can reach into your physical being and fix it with tender, loving care. He is the only Man who can read your thoughts and know your deepest desires. His perfect love casts out all fear.

Are you looking for a man to be your provider? [Page 60, I learned to take God at His word: He is my Husband and He will take care of me.] Sometimes God will provide right away and sometimes He will make you wait because He knows your heart. He knows that you can say you trust Him, but if you are really lying to yourself and to Him, then He will make you wait so that you can get totally honest with Him (the prayer-convince process again).

Are you looking for a man to be your best friend? [Page 64] Who could be a better friend than someone who loved you first, gave His life for you, provides for you, teaches you, guides your every step, and has only your best interest at heart?

The Lord Almighty is His name. [Page 66] This is the name God gives us in Isaiah 54:5. In the original Hebrew, according to Strong's concordance, it is "Jehovah Sabaoth." Jehovah meaning "Lord" or "I AM." Sabaoth means "hosts or armies." God is introducing Himself to you as the Lord Almighty. This name implies a military organization, an organization designed for war. God is the Lord of the heavenly Armies!

He is the Supreme Commander, the General of the Army. And this Lord of Hosts is your Husband! Why does He use this name in this verse to introduce Himself? He uses this name here and now because we need Him to be the Lord of Hosts here and now (remember your fear/need lists?). He is telling you that He is your Knight in Shining Armor!

The Holy One of Israel is your Redeemer. [Page 67] God is telling you what He does for a living: He redeems, He rescues, and restores. What would a Knight in Shining Armor do for a living? Why, rescue damsels in distress, of course!

He is called the God of all the earth. [Page 69] This is God's title, the God of the Whole Earth. The heaven is His throne and the earth is His footstool. His feet are here on earth; He walks with you and is here with you. He is ready here and now to help you and rescue you.

Session Two: Lessons 3 and 4

LESSON 4: I AM A PATIENT MAN 15 minutes

We have now been formally introduced to God. We know His name, the LORD of Hosts; His job, to redeem and rescue; and His title, the God of all the Earth.

Read Isaiah 54:6, page 71, and also in the New King James Version, page 72.

God identifies you in the midst of your situation. He knows stuff about you that know one else knows. Isn't it easier to trust someone who already knows all about you?

God is sharing your experiences with you. [Page 71] He is telling you that He knows who you are.

He knows that we are women who are forsaken, have been forsaken, will be forsaken, or just feel like we are forsaken. We are not only forsaken but we are also grieved in spirit.

God is telling you that He knows this. He knows the deepest hurts of your heart. He is telling you that He knows so that you can begin to trust Him to heal you.

God is telling you that He knows your past and any and all hurts or wrongs done to you when you were young. Some of these hurts can last a lifetime but He wants you to be healed and free.

God wants you to surrender these hurts to Him so that you will not have to live with them for the rest of your life. He wants you to live with Him for the rest of your life.

He says He is your God. [Page 76] He is your very own. He wants to belong to you.

Read Isaiah 54:7, page 78.

God will choose to reveal some of His character to you when you are in a bad situation. It gives you the best opportunity to know Him better. He knows that any bad situation will really only last a little while, and you need to trust Him for that.

Sometimes it feels like God has abandoned you, [Page 79] and that God is not listening to you. There are two reasons why God does this. First, you get to know yourself better, and second, you get to know God better. Your true character comes out in bad situations, and they test whether or not you really trust God. Pay attention to what true character traits are coming out in you and pay attention when God reveals His character.

Usually we find out how prideful or self-centered we are when things do not go our own way.

Humble yourself when you ask God for help and He will begin to reveal His true character to you.

God will reveal His patience and compassion. [Page 83] He is like a father watching His baby girl take her first steps. She may falter or even fall down, but He does not reach out to help her unless to prevent injury. She needs to learn that she can walk, and learn that God really is there to help her if she needs it.

God has introduced Himself to you: He is the Lord Almighty, come to rescue and redeem you.

He is the God of all the earth; He is here now and all things are in His control.

He is patient and compassionate and He really does love you and He really will not let you come to harm, if you surrender to Him.

Pray the prayer on page 85 together.

Ministry Time/Closing Prayer.

Session Three: Lessons 5, 6, and 7

Opening Prayer 1 to 2 minutes

Lesson 3 Discussion Questions 20 minutes

    a. Question #3, page 54

    b. Question #5, page 61, read the scripture, then answer the question.

Lesson 4 Discussion Questions 20 minutes

    a. Question #2, page 74

    b. Question #4, page 80, read the scriptures, then answer the question.

Teaching

LESSON 5: I AM A REAL MAN 15 minutes

Read Isaiah 54:8, page 87.

We have learned God's name, His job, His title and some aspects of His character. He is the Lord of Hosts, the General of the Army, and your husband. His job is to rescue and redeem you. He is the God of all the earth who is patient and compassionate.

Verse 8 reveals how God reacts to some situations. When you are in a bad situation, God knows all about it. He may be angry about it. He is reacting to whatever is going on in your life.

This word "anger" or "wrath" means "cracked" or "splintered." Something bad may have happened suddenly and God is reacting to it. He is showing you how He reacts to some situations.

There is usually only one reason why God gets angry. That is because of sin. It does not matter whose. Sin causes bad situations. God gets angry because He knows what consequences there will be because of sin.

But He is only a little angry towards you and your situation. [Page 88] It may seem like a lot of anger towards you sometimes, especially when you think He is not listening to you.

But God promises that His anger will only last a moment. In the perspective of time, it really is only for a little while.

He promises to show you everlasting kindness and turn His face towards you again. [Page 90] God has said He is your husband and you can live "happily ever after" with Him, just like in a fairy tale! He really does love you!

His kindness will last forever! Not just in heaven, but here and now.

There are four different character qualities that God reveals to us in this verse. [Isaiah 54:8]

1. **The first quality is "everlasting."** He shows you that He is entirely capable of being steadfast, faithful, and true. He may appear to "forsake" you at times, but He never really will. He will never leave you.

2. **The second quality is "kindness."** He is capable of showing His beauty and His favor. He may show anger sometimes, but He will also show His

kindness. **If you are in a bad situation, would you want the person who is rescuing you to be incapable of anger?** It is God's love that fuels His righteous anger and, in turn, compels Him to rescue you.

3. **The third quality is wrapped up in the word "mercy."** This word in the original Hebrew, according to Strong's concordance, implies, "to find, or obtain." **God is persistent and not a quitter.** He will do whatever it takes to have mercy on you.

4. **The fourth quality is mercy itself.** God is a Man who is capable of great tenderness and great feeling. Here is a Man who is not afraid to show His sensitive side.

LESSON 6: I HURT WHEN YOU HURT   15 minutes

Read Isaiah 54:9, page 95.

What is "this?" "This" is whatever bad situation you are in. God acknowledges that He knows how bad it is.

In fact, He thinks any bad situation you are in is just as bad as when the Great Flood happened. This is how He feels about it. He takes it very seriously!

God is reminding you that He really does know and understand whatever it is that you are going through. He is just as grieved, or more so, over whatever destruction has occurred or is occurring in your life.

God is worried. He is feeling pain and anger. He is hurt and He is sorry. God is revealing His heart to you and He is now showing you His emotions. He is not just showing His reactions to the situation. He is now showing you His emotions and how He feels.

Then God remembers His covenant with Noah, and He now applies it to your situations. [Page 99]

He repeats His oath. He will not rebuke you, nor be angry with you.

He is revealing His character, His reactions, and His emotions to you so that you can know Him better and so you will want to surrender to Him.

LESSON 7: I KEEP MY PROMISES   15 minutes

Read Isaiah 54:10, page 101.

God reminds you that change is inevitable. Even the earth itself, and all the people, things, and places in it, will change.

Change is difficult, scary, and can make us feel very insecure. We may have to make changes that affect our lives permanently.

One thing does not change; that is, only one Person does not change. [Page 103] Malachi 3:6, He is the LORD, and He does not change. If security is to be found in someone or something that does not change, then only God is that Someone.

His unfailing love for you will not be shaken. [Page 104] His kindness, His love, His compassion, and His patience will never change!

Unfailing love is obviously love that never fails, love that never gives up. His is a love that is always there with beauty, favor, and mercy. His is a love that is there through thick and thin. His is a love that will lead you out of your dark places or bad circumstances. His is a love that will wrap you up and shelter you.

His is a love that will hold you, comfort you, and be with you forever and ever.

God has made a covenant, a vow, a promise. [Page 105] He makes a covenant of peace with you. You will have peace when you know who He really is. You will have peace when you know that you can trust Him to love you and take care of you forever and ever.

Pray the prayer on page 107 together.
Ministry Time/Closing Prayer.

Session Four: Lessons 8, 9, 10, and 11

Opening Prayer   1 to 2 minutes

Lesson 5 Discussion Questions   15 minutes

    a. Question #3, page 89, read the scriptures, then answer the question.

    b. Question #5, page 93, read the scriptures, then answer the question.

Lesson 6 Discussion Question   10 minutes

    a. Question #2, page 97.

Lesson 7 Discussion Questions   15 minutes

    a. Question #1, page 102.

    b. Question #5, page 108.

Teaching

    Read the seven aspects of God's character on pages 195 and 196. [Numbers 1 through 7, as a summary to remind the women what they have already learned.]

In Isaiah 54, verses 11, 12, and 13, God makes seven statements that we are to believe.

God says He will lay stones, build foundations, install windows, install doors, build borders; not literally, but figuratively in your lives. He will teach your children, and give your family peace.

LESSON 8: I WILL LAY BEAUTIFUL STONES

Read Isaiah 54:11

First of all, God calls us an "afflicted city." You may be afflicted by some situation or circumstance, poor judgment on your part, or just emotional issues you may have due to your upbringing or personality.

"I will lay beautiful stones" [Page 115] Stones are an underlayment of foundations. When God begins to go to work on us, as we surrender more and more to Him, He begins by laying stones, or replacing broken stones, or filling in the holes in our lives.

Session Four: Lessons 8, 9, 10, and 11

These "stones" can represent anger, rebellion, rejection, depression, and the list goes on and on. Can you give some more examples? [Give the women a few minutes to answer this question.]

Whatever issues you have in your life, that are not part of the personality that God created in you, may have to be fixed, repaired, made, or replaced. God will replace these ugly "stones" with beautiful stones. Read Galatians 5:22-23, for a list of the fruits of the Spirit, the most beautiful "stones."

Believe God when He says He will lay beautiful stones in your life when you surrender to Him.

Pray the prayer on page 117 together.

LESSON 9: I WILL LAY FOUNDATIONS 5 minutes

Once God has begun to replace or mend our "stones," He moves on to build new foundations in our lives. A foundation is built on top of the stones, those parts that have been replaced or repaired. A foundation is the very beginning of a beautiful structure that God will build out of your life.

He will "establish, instruct, lay, and ordain" your self. You are to be instructed and established by His word. You need to be in His word everyday, learning from Him, and letting Him build a strong, beautiful foundation on Him in order to have the security and peace you desire. [According to Strong's concordance, this word "foundation" means "to be established, instructed, laid, and ordained."]

These foundations will be strong like sapphires or diamonds: a gem for scratching other stones. We need strong foundations so that we cannot be moved by winds of change, emotions, or circumstances. [Again, according to Strong's, the word sapphire means a "gem for scratching other stones." This sounds like a diamond to me, since diamonds cannot be scratched. Just what we need to be made of: something that cannot be scratched.]

Session Four: Lessons 8, 9, 10, and 11

We need foundations that are built by God to be secure in Him when the winds and storms blow in our lives. If you have a foundation made of diamond, would you ever be "scratched" or affected by circumstances or by others?

Believe God when He says that He will build you with strong foundations when you are growing in Him.

Pray the prayer on page 119 together.

LESSON 10: I WILL PUT IN WINDOWS 10 minutes

Read Isaiah 54:12 on page 123.

God will "put in windows." Trust God as He builds you and makes you new. After replacing your stones and building a new foundation in you, now God will put in windows. [This is exactly how houses and buildings are really made: first the stones, then the foundation, then the windows, and then the doors.]

Trust God when He brings or allows storms to lash about you that will make you cling to Him even more. When the going gets tough, grab hold of Jesus!

This word "window," in the Hebrew, means a notched battlement or window. A battlement is an opening designed for defense. You can see out of it as well as use weapons to protect yourself from attack. Think of a castle window: thin, narrow, and thick walled. Most castles are still standing today because they were built strong and thick.

God is in the business of establishing and building us into something beautiful. Picture what He has built already, your stones of turquoise, your foundations of sapphires or diamonds, and now battlements or windows of rubies. Wow, what a structure!

The more you allow Him to mold you, shape you, and do His will, the more beautiful you will become, the stronger you will become, and the more secure you will become. You will not only be strong, but gorgeous as well when you surrender all to Jesus Christ.

Believe God when He says that He will make you into someone that will be able to withstand attack.

Session Four: Lessons 8, 9, 10, and 11

LESSON 11: I WILL INSTALL DOORS   10 minutes

After the windows are installed, God will put in the doors to your life. These doors, or gates, match the windows: they are made of sparkling jewels, possibly rubies, and not only are beautiful to look at, but useful as well.

A door or gate works two ways. You can let yourself out, or you can let others in. This part that God is building in you refers to your openness and vulnerability. God will help you be more open and honest with yourself, and with others. He will teach you how to be vulnerable but not weak because you are strong in Him.

How open are you with others? Can you share your faith, or your testimony easily? God wants you to be able to. He wants you to be honest and free with your self toward others, yet confident and secure in Him.

Or how about letting others in? Do you trust other people or do you keep everyone at a distance away from your true self. This defensive posture can be caused by fear of rejection.

Remember chapter 1? NO FEAR! Do not be afraid to let others into your life, with wisdom, of course. And do not be afraid to be yourself with whomever you are with. God does not want you to wear a mask that hides your true self.

God will, when you surrender to His work in your life, build your structure into one of magnificence.

Imagine being so secure in God that you are not moved by circumstances or other people or what others think of you. Imagine resting in Him so that you are who you are all the time, no plastic smile or face trying to hide the real you for fear of rejection.

Remember who loves you! Remember who is romancing you! The Living God, The Ancient of Days, the King of all Kings, the Lord of Hosts, Your Husband and Your Redeemer!

Session Four: Lessons 8, 9, 10, and 11

Now what in the world is there to be afraid of?

Believe God when He says that He will make you into a person who is not afraid to open her doors.

Ministry Time/Closing Prayer.

Session Five: Lessons 12, 13, and 14

Opening Prayer   1 to 2 minutes

Lesson 8 Discussion Questions   10 minutes

    a. Question #2, page 114.

    b. Question #3, page 117.

Lesson 10 Discussion Question   10 minutes

    a. Question #1, page 125, read scriptures, then answer the question.

Lesson 11 Discussion Question   10 minutes

    a. Question #2, page 130.

Teaching

    God is in the middle of fixing, repairing, or building us anew. He is building foundations, and putting in windows and doors. He is building you into a beautiful new structure that will stand and be with Him forever.

LESSON 12: I WILL BUILD WALLS   15 minutes

    Read Isaiah 54:12, page 131.

God is going to build walls, borders, or fences. These are the borders of your property. While you are the property and God is the owner, these borders will define you and landscape you. [Page 131, according to Strong's concordance, the word used here means a cord that ropes off and encloses a territory or space.]

You can look out of your windows onto the world without others seeing you. You can open yourself up to others by going in and out of your doors, but a border or fence is always there for others to see. It is the part of you that everyone always sees.

God is going to build these borders out of precious stones. Precious means "pleasure or desire," "valuable," or "delightful," according to Webster. These are the parts of you, that when others see how beautiful and secure you are, they will want to be built like you are—by a God who loves them.

Session Five: Lessons 12, 13, and 14

Believe God when He tells you that you will be beautiful on the outside, for all others to see.

LESSON 13: I WILL TEACH YOUR CHILIDREN

Read Isaiah 54:13, page 135.

The final two things that God says for us to believe have to do with the very things that are closest to our hearts: our children and our families.

God says He will teach your children. Children in the context of this scripture refers to all children. So, they could be your literal, biological children, children given into your care, or your spiritual children. [I want to include all types of children: our own birth children, someone else's birth children, or "children" who we have responsibility for such as brothers, sisters, friends, or co-workers.]

Who are your spiritual children? They are your relatives, family, friends, and co-workers.

The broad sense of this term, "children," basically can refer to anyone close to you. Your "child" is anyone over whom you have influence or upon whom you have a positive impact.

These are the people God has placed in your life so that you will have an effect on them for His purposes.

God wants them all to be taught by and of Him. And this means by you! Most of the time God uses people to do His work and that includes teaching and influencing people. And as you come into your new, secure, loved self, you really will be able to shine in their lives.

LESSON 14: I WILL GIVE YOUR FAMILY PEACE

God's last promise to believe is that He will give your family peace. So many families do not have peace. There can be continual fighting and bickering, and even estrangement between family members.

God wants our families to have peace. He wants us to have peace.

He wants to build you in such a way that He can use you as an instrument for peace in your family. This is a promise that God will not only use you, but that He will keep His promise to you about your family.

Surrender your family to God and then hang on to this promise!

This concludes the seven promises that God makes to us.

Ministry Time/Closing Prayer

Session Six: Lessons 15, 16, and 17

Opening Prayer   1 to 2 minutes

Lesson 13 Discussion Questions   30 minutes

    a. Question #1, page 136. Read Hebrews 11:17-19, then answer the question.

    b. Question #2, page 137.

    c. Question #3, page 138.

Teaching

LESSON 15: YOU CAN HAVE PEACE   10 minutes

    Read the Believe Summary on page 196 and 197.

[Numbers 1 through 7, as a summary to remind the women what to believe.]

    Read Isaiah 54:14, page 147.

    We are being established in righteousness. "Righteousness" generally means "in right standing with God." God is the one who will establish us in His right standing.

Nothing we do will ever cause us to be in right standing with God. His Son, Jesus Christ, paid for it all on the cross.

There are two aspects of righteousness with God. We are in the righteousness of Jesus Christ automatically when we first receive Him as our Lord and Savior.

Then there is the righteousness that we grow into as we grow spiritually. This is the righteousness that we live in day to day.

Peace is only found by doing things God's way. [Page 148] Let God establish you in His righteousness by believing that He can take care of you.

Begin to let go of trusting your own feelings and emotions.

To be established in God's righteousness you need to realize [Page 149]:

1. You cannot get to Heaven on your own no matter what you do.

2. You cannot, very easily, change your patterns, behaviors, and habits by yourself.

3. You cannot change others at all.

4. You can only affect your own decisions.

Let God change you. Let God affect you. Let God be in control. Let God establish you, then you will have His peace.

LESSON 16: YOU CAN BE FREE   20 minutes

Read Isaiah 54:14, page 153.

According to Webster, tyranny is "unjust or cruel exercise of authority." God promises that tyranny will be far from you.

People, circumstances, and life can be unfair, cruel, and unjust.

God says you will be free! You can be free from Fear, Worry, and Bad Habits.

Read John 8:31, 32.

Jesus said we will know the truth. But, the question is not "what is truth." The question is "Who is Truth."

Read John 14:6, 7. Jesus himself said we will know the truth and then He turns around and says that He is the truth. Do you want truth in your life? Then seek Jesus Christ!

We will have freedom when we surrender to the Truth, Jesus Christ.

What do you need to be free of?

Substance abuse is one of the biggest problems in the world today. [Page 154] People use substances to try to find peace and security. In fact, they are only masking or drowning their problems and the peace and security they think they have found only lasts a little while, until they are sober or straight again. [Some people say Jesus is a crutch. Well, I would much rather have Jesus for a crutch than any substance.]

Anger and violence are becoming more and more prevalent these days. [Page 156] Step back and think why you get angry. What do you get angry about and why? Isn't it really because you did not get your own way? For example, if someone cuts you off in traffic, don't you get angry at them because now you are a few feet further behind, you had to slam on the brakes, and now you will be a second later to your appointment? [Ask the women to come up with more examples to share and see if this observation is correct: they did not get their own way.] **Did Jesus always get His own way? No, He laid His own life down for others every day!**

Are you a "doormat" for others? [Page 160] Do you let others take advantage of you only to get angry about the situation later? Why do you let them take advantage of you? There is a difference between being selfless and being a doormat. Selfless is serving others because it is the right thing do, what Jesus would do, when others need help. A "doormat" mentality yields the will and personality for the sake of being liked, loved, or accepted by others. **God does**

not want you to be a doormat, though He does want you to be selfless.

Fear of rejection; almost everyone in the world has this problem. [Page 162] When you understand how much the Master loves you (as much as you can), then you will be free from the fear of rejection. Part of overcoming fear of rejection is realizing that the only thing that really matters in life, the universe, and everything is that Jesus loves you!

The next part of overcoming a fear of rejection is to recognize a spirit of rejection and learn to starve it. A spirit of rejection feeds on rejection. It can put thoughts or ideas into your head that you may act on with the result that you are rejected by others and then you wonder why. Learn to recognize these thoughts or ideas and follow their end before you act them out or say them. Then, you can stop doing or saying things that would cause others to reject you, and thereby starve the spirit.

Session Six: Lessons 15, 16, and 17

Learn to recognize this pattern in order to break it. [Cleansing Stream Ministries deals in depth with rejection and how to be free from it. Also, encourage the women to get prayer from people who know how to pray for this issue.]

What do you think about your appearance? [Page 165] There are two ends to this issue: one is being totally obsessed with your appearance to the point that no one ever sees you not made up and dressed; the other is not caring about what you look like, no matter where you go or what you do. Both of these can be caused by fear or poor self-image.

When you know how much the Master loves you, and that He made you just the way you are, then you can have the peace, security, and freedom that comes with the balance that God can give you regarding your appearance.

These are just a few issues that can keep us in bondage. [Ask the women if they have any other ideas about other issues that can be addressed here.]

LESSON 17: YOU ARE LOVED   10 minutes

You will have nothing to fear. Refer back to 1 John 4:18: perfect love casts out fear. When you know the Master's perfect love you will have nothing to fear.

In Lesson 1, "Fear not" was a command. In this verse, Isaiah 54:14, it is now a promise that we will not fear.

God now makes this promise that we will have no fear because:

1. We are getting to know Him better.
2. We are beginning to believe Him.
3. We are letting Him work in us and build us and fix us.
4. We receive His kindness, compassion, mercy, and most of all, His wonderful love.

We are learning to place our confidence in Him. Our confidence comes from Him when we are surrendered to Him and know how much He loves us.

Read the last sentence on page 171 together.

Session Six: Lessons 15, 16, and 17

Ministry Time/Closing Prayer

Session Seven: Lessons 18, 19, 20, and 21

Opening Prayer   1 to 2 minutes

Lesson 15 Discussion Questions   10 minutes

    a. Question #2, page 150.

    b. Question #3, page 150.

Lesson 16 Discussion Questions   30 minutes

    a. Question #2, page 156, read the scriptures, then answer the question.

    b. Question #4, page 159, read the scripture, then answer the question.

    c. Question #5, page 159, read the scripture, then answer the question.

    d. Question #6, page 161, read the scriptures, then answer the question.

    e. Question #9, page 167.

A Romance With the Master: Teaching Guide

Lesson 17 Discussion Question 10 minutes

a. Question #1, page 170, read the scripture, then answer the question.

Teaching

LESSON 18: YOU CAN LIVE IN SAFETY

Read Isaiah 54:14, page 173.

Terror will not come near you. God is promising that we no longer have to live in a state of intense fear, about anything, ever. [Webster says "a state of intense fear" is the definition of "terror."]

When our trust is in God, then our deep, inner being does not have to be afraid of anything in the midst of any circumstances anymore.

This verse is not necessarily promising that no more bad things will happen to you. It is promising that when your security is in God and your eyes and heart are stayed on Him, then there will be no more terror for you.

Session Seven: Lessons 18, 19, 20, and 21

This verse is promising *inner* safety and security when you cling to God. [You may want to read my testimony about cancer on pages 173 and 174. Or you may have a testimony to share on this topic.]

Read the scriptures, Romans 8:31-39, on pages 174 and 175. [Get the women to discuss their most terrifying thoughts or moments and use Paul's example to dispel their terror.]

LESSON 19: YOU CAN BE STRONG   10 minutes

Read Isaiah 54:15, page 177.

God makes the promise of no more terror because He knows that we will be attacked in this life and on this earth.

He wants us to be secure in Him and in His love for us so that we can withstand the attacks.

Attacks can be physical, mental, emotional, spiritual, or verbal [Page 177]. They will usually come through other people, though the enemy is not above attacking you directly.

Attacks are designed to weaken us, shake our confidence, and cause us to doubt what God is doing.

Read John 10:10. [Have the women discuss the work of the enemy. Also have them contrast that with what Jesus says He came to do (same verse).]

This verse reminds us of the real world. When the attacks come, remember in Whom you trust!

He is the God of the Whole Earth, the Lord of Hosts, your Redeemer, and your Husband who loves you more than anyone ever can or will! [Page 178]

When the attacks come remember that our God is a God of Battles. He is the General of the Army and the Great Military Commander! He will fight for you!

Now you can trust that God will be your strength and He will cause whomever or whatever attacks you to surrender [Page 179].

Session Seven: Lessons 18, 19, 20, and 21

LESSON 20: YOU CAN BE CLEAN   10 minutes

Read Isaiah 54:16, page 181.

There are four things you should know about the attacks that come your way [Page 181]:

1. God does not plan them.
2. God does allow them.
3. The attacks will ultimately serve a divine purpose.
4. The attacks will never overtake you, or destroy you, or be more than you can handle.

We live in a fallen world where good things happen to "bad" people and bad things happen to "good" people. That is why there is no guarantee that we will not be attacked, or that bad things will not happen to us.

But we do know the Master who is in control of everything; who sees it all and knows it all. Trust Him when you are feeling the pressure and are under attack.

How many attacks can you handle? Trust God to know your true limit. You may feel like you are at the end of your rope, but only God can see where the end of the rope really is.

Why the picture of a blacksmith making weapons? [Page 183] Because God created everything, even the enemy. It is an accurate picture of how we can be molded, shaped, and refined even though the process may hurt.

And just like steel or iron being forged into a weapon, we can feel like we are in the fire, pounded, molded, drowned, or squeezed when we are under attack.

There two reasons why God allows an attack:

1. God allows an attack to get our attention. When things are going well, do we always remember Him?
2. God allows an attack because it softens us and gets us ready for His molding and shaping.

Fire is the true test of character. [Page 184] Again, pay attention to the character that comes out of you when you are "in the fire." Pay attention to God's character during an attack; watch for Him to be working.

We do not surrender to the attack and give up; we surrender to God!

Surrender to God to find your peace, freedom, love, safety, and strength!

God is in control. [Page 186] God is always in control even if you do not quite believe He is. In the midst of an attack is when your knowledge of His character, your belief in what He says, and your trust in Him needs to kick in.

LESSON 21: YOU CAN BE INVINCIBLE

Read Isaiah 54:17, page 189.

The attacks will come, but no weapon forged against you shall prevail! This is God's promise to you!

We can be invincible because we are at peace, we are free, we are loved, we are safe, we are strong, and we are clean. We can rest in all that God has done and is doing for us.

When we rest, we are invincible! [Page 189] When we are surrendered to God to the best of our ability, then we are shielded from any attacks or weapons against us.

We are invincible because it is our God who fights for us!

We are shielded and invincible through His strength alone [Page 190].

Three incredible results of surrender [Page 192]:

1. We have the authority to refute judging remarks against us.
2. We have confidence that we will not be shaken.
3. We have assurance: self-assurance and God-assurance.

These three things constitute the ultimate security in God.

You can have the freedom and confidence to be the woman God made you to be.

You can have authority because it is the authority God gives you because of your trust in Him.

You can have assurance because you know that God will do what He says He will do.

We can be secure because God has made us part of His family. We are daughters of God and joint-Heirs with Christ. We are His children now that we have surrendered all to Him!

We are His servants, serving the Good Master who always takes care of His servants.

God has just declared all of this! He loves you, He wants you, He cares for you, and He wants to romance you more than ever. Know, Believe, and Trust Him with all of your heart!

Ministry Time/Closing Prayer

Session Eight: Final Discussion

Opening Prayer　　　　　　　　　　1 to 2 minutes

Read the Trust Summary on page 197. [Numbers 1 through 7, as a summary to remind the women what they learned about trust.]

Lesson 18 Discussion Question　　　　10 minutes

    a. Question #1, page 176.

Lesson 19 Discussion Questions　　　　20 minutes

    a. Question #1, page 178 [It was suggested to discuss this question during the teaching of Lesson 19. If it was not, then do it here, or discuss it again.]

    b. Question #2, page 179.

Lesson 20 Discussion Questions　　　　30 minutes

    a. Question #1, page 182, read the scriptures, then answer the question.

    b. Question #3, page 186, read the scriptures, then answer the question.

A Romance With the Master: Teaching Guide

    c. Question #4, page 187.

Lesson 21 Discussion Questions　　　　　　20 minutes

    a. Question #1, page 189, read the scriptures and share thoughts about them.

    b. Question #2, page 193, read the scriptures, then answer the question.

Any further discussion of your choice.

Ministry Time/Closing Prayer

SCHEDULE KAREN D. GREENWELL

FOR CONFERENCES, RETREATS, SEMINARS,

BOOK SIGNINGS AND OTHER SPECIAL EVENTS

AT:

HTTP://WWW.HIGGINSPUBLISHING.COM

IF THIS TEACHING GUIDE HAS BEEN A BLESSING TO YOU,

PLEASE SUBMIT A REVIEW ONLINE

AT YOUR FAVORITE ONLINE BOOKSTORE.

THANK YOU FOR TAKING THE TIME

TO LET US KNOW

HOW YOU ENJOYED THIS TEACHING GUIDE.

HIGGINS PUBLISHING

WWW.HIGGINSPUBLISHING.COM

PHONE: (510) 431-6832

www.ingramcontent.com/pod-product-compliance
Lightning Source LLC
Chambersburg PA
CBHW071538080526
44588CB00011B/1721